EXCELLENCE

EXCELLENCE

Edited by Jill Wolf

ISBN 0-89954-441-X
Copyright © 1992 Antioch Publishing Company
Yellow Springs, Ohio 45387

Printed in the U.S.A.

CONTENTS

*One that desires to excel should endeavor
it in those things that are in
themselves most excellent.*

—Epictetus

*To be and remain true to oneself and others
is to possess the noblest attribute
of the greatest talents.*

—Johann Wolfgang von Goethe

*It is the greatest of all mistakes to do nothing
because you can only do a little.
Do what you can.*

—Sydney Smith

*Nothing great was ever achieved
without enthusiasm.*
            —Ralph Waldo Emerson

*Ordinary people merely think how they shall spend
their time; a man of talent tries to use it.*
                —Arthur Schopenhauer

The secret of success is constancy to purpose.
                —Benjamin Disraeli

HIGHER GOALS

One that desires to excel should endeavor it in those things that are in themselves most excellent.

—*Epictetus*

...whatever is true, whatever is noble, whatever is right, whatever is pure, whatever is lovely, whatever is admirable—if anything is excellent or praiseworthy—think about such things.

Philippians 4:8 (NIV)

We needs must love the highest when we see it.

—*Alfred, Lord Tennyson*

Love of truth shows itself in this, that a man knows how to find and value the good in everything.

—*Johann Wolfgang von Goethe*

Great God, I ask Thee for no meaner pelf
Than that I may not disappoint myself;
That in my action I may soar as high
As I can now discern with this clear eye.
—*Henry David Thoreau*

O Lord...I am Thy servant, prepared for all
things: I desire not to live unto myself, but unto
Thee; and oh, that I could do it worthily and
perfectly!
—*Thomas à Kempis*

Ah, but a man's reach should exceed his grasp,
Or what's a heaven for?
—*Robert Browning*

To produce a mighty book, you must choose a
mighty theme.
—*Herman Melville*

Hitch your wagon to a star.
—*Ralph Waldo Emerson*

The true worth of a man is to be measured by the objects he pursues.

—*Marcus Aurelius*

In the long run, men hit only what they aim at. Therefore...they had better aim at something high.

—*Henry David Thoreau*

Greatly begin! though thou have time
But for a line, be that sublime,—
Not failure, but low aim is crime.

—*James Russell Lowell*

Do not pray for easy lives; pray to be stronger men. Do not pray for tasks equal to your powers; pray for powers equal to your tasks. Then the doing of your work shall be no miracle, but you shall be a miracle. Every day you shall wonder at yourself, at the richness of life which has come to you by the grace of God.

—*Phillips Brooks*

Excellence is the perfect excuse.
> —*Ralph Waldo Emerson*

There is only one real failure in life, and that is not to be true to the best one knows.
> —*Frederic W. Farrar*

Did you ever hear of a man who had striven all his life faithfully and singly toward an object and in no measure obtained it? If a man constantly aspires, is he not elevated?
> —*Henry David Thoreau*

Bad will be the day for every man when he becomes absolutely contented with the life that he is living, with the thoughts that he is thinking, with the deeds that he is doing, when there is not forever beating at the doors of his soul some great desire to do something larger, which he knows that he was meant and made to do because he is still, in spite of all, the child of God.
> —*Phillips Brooks*

Show me a thoroughly satisfied man, and I will show you a failure.

—*Thomas A. Edison*

There are one-story intellects, two-story intellects, and three-story intellects with sky-lights. All fact collectors, who have no aim beyond their facts, are one-story men. Two-story men compare, reason, generalize, using the labors of the fact collectors as well as their own. Three-story men idealize, imagine, predict; their best illumination comes from above, through the skylight.

—*Oliver Wendell Holmes*

The rung of a ladder was never meant to rest upon, but only to hold a man's foot long enough to enable him to put the other some-what higher.

—*Thomas H. Huxley*

I find the great thing in this world is not so much where we stand as in what direction we are moving.

—Oliver Wendell Holmes

We never know how high we are
Till we are called to rise;
And then, if we are true to plan,
Our statures touch the skies.

—Emily Dickinson

Life is no brief candle to me. It is a sort of splendid torch which I have got hold of for the moment, and I want to make it burn as brightly as possible before handing it on to future generations.

—George Bernard Shaw

Whatever is worth doing at all, is worth doing well.

—Philip Dormer Stanhope

EXCELLENCE

Excellence is dedication
To a job that's hard to do,
Going the extra mile
And always trying to follow through.

Excellence is communication,
Sharing everything you know,
And learning how to listen
So your expertise will grow.

Excellence is appreciation
Of the talent that you see,
Acknowledging a job well done
Inspires success and loyalty.

Excellence is aspiration
With a higher goal in mind,
To trust in God and reach for things
Of a more rewarding kind.

—Jill Wolf

Do all the good you can,
By all the means you can,
In all the ways you can,
In all the places you can,
At all the times you can,
To all the people you can,
As long as ever you can.
—John Wesley

We are here to add what we can to, not to get
what we can from, life.
—Sir William Osler

Be not simply good; be good for something.
—Henry David Thoreau

The great use of life is to spend it for something that outlasts it.
—William James

Every soul that touches yours—
Be it the slightest contact—
Gets therefrom some good;
Some little grace; one kindly thought;
One aspiration yet unfelt;
One bit of courage
For the darkening sky;
One gleam of faith
To brave the thickening ills of life;
One glimpse of brighter skies—
To make this life worthwhile
And heaven a surer heritage.

—George Eliot

If a man measures life by what others do for
him, he is apt to be disappointed; but if he
measures life by what he does for others, there
is no time for despair.

—William Jennings Bryan

That best portion of a good man's life,—
His little, nameless, unremembered acts
Of kindness and love.

—William Wordsworth

I live for those who love me, for those
    who know me true;
For the heaven that smiles above me,
    and awaits my spirit too;
For the cause that lacks assistance, for the
    wrong that needs resistance,
For the future in the distance, and the good
    that I can do.

—George Linnaeus Banks

Die when I may, I want it said of me by those
who knew me best, that I always plucked a
thistle and planted a flower where I thought a
flower would grow.

—Abraham Lincoln

If you have knowledge, let others light their
candles at it.

—Thomas Fuller

The most important single ingredient in the
formula of success is the knack of getting
along with people.

—Theodore Roosevelt

Every man is said to have his peculiar ambition. Whether it be true or not, I can say, for one, that I have no other so great as that of being truly esteemed of my fellow-men, by rendering myself worthy of their esteem.

—*Abraham Lincoln*

That man is a success who has lived well, laughed often and loved much; who has gained the respect of intelligent men and the love of children; who has filled his niche and accomplished his task; who leaves the world better than he found it, whether by an improved poppy, a perfect poem or a rescued soul; who never lacked appreciation of earth's beauty or failed to express it; who looked for the best in others and gave the best he had.

—*Robert Louis Stevenson*

To be honest, to be kind; to earn a little and to spend a little less; to make upon the whole a family happier for his presence; to renounce when that shall be necessary and not to be embittered; to keep a few friends, but those without capitulation; above all, on the same grim conditions, to keep friends with himself— here is a task for all that man has of fortitude and delicacy.

—Robert Louis Stevenson

To awaken each morning with a smile brightening my face; to greet the day with reverence for the opportunities it contains; to approach my work with a clean mind; to hold ever before me, even in the doing of little things, the Ultimate Purpose toward which I am working; to meet men and women with laughter on my lips and love in my heart; to be gentle, kind, and courteous through all the hours; to approach the night with weariness that ever woos sleep, and the joy that comes from work well done—this is how I desire to waste wisely my days.

—Thomas Dekker

REST

Rest is not quitting
The busy career,
Rest is the fitting
Of self to its sphere.

'Tis the brook's motion,
Clear without strife,
Fleeing to ocean,
After its life.

'Tis loving and serving,
The Highest and Best;
'Tis onwards! unswerving,
And that is true rest.

—John Sullivan Dwight

BEING TRUE TO YOURSELF

The first step to greatness is to be honest.
—Samuel Johnson

The first and last thing that is required of genius is love of truth.
—Johann Wolfgang von Goethe

No man can produce great things who is not thoroughly sincere in dealing with himself.
—James Russell Lowell

To be and remain true to oneself and others is to possess the noblest attribute of the greatest talents.
—Johann Wolfgang von Goethe

Be true to your own highest convictions.
—William Ellery Channing

Never esteem anything as of advantage to thee that shall make thee break thy word or lose thy self-respect.

—Marcus Aurelius

Public opinion is a weak tyrant compared with our own private opinion. What a man thinks of himself, that it is which determines, or rather indicates, his fate.

—Henry David Thoreau

I call that mind free which is not passively framed by outward circumstances, which is not swept away by the torrent of events, which is not the creature of accidental impulse, but which bends events to its own improvement, and acts from an inward spring, from immutable principles which it has deliberately espoused.

—William Ellery Channing

He is wisest, who only gives,
True to himself, the best he can:
Who drifting on the winds of praise,
The inward monitor obeys.
And with the boldness that confuses fear
Takes in the crowded sail, and lets
    his conscience steer.

—*John Greenleaf Whittier*

Whatever you are by nature, keep to it; never
desert your line of talent. Be what nature
intended you for, and you will succeed.

—*Sydney Smith*

There is a kind of greatness which does not
depend upon fortune; it is a certain manner that
distinguishes us, and which seems to destine us
for great things; it is the value we insensibly set
upon ourselves; it is by this quality that we gain
the deference of other men, and it is this which
commonly raises us more above them than
birth, rank, or even merit itself.

—*La Rochefoucauld*

To be what we are, and to become what we are capable of becoming, is the only end of life.

—Robert Louis Stevenson

The highest reward for man's toil is not what he gets for it but what he becomes by it.

—John Ruskin

Of all paths a man could strike into, there is, at any given moment, a *best path* for every man; a thing which, here and now, it were of all things *wisest* for him to do; which could he but be led or driven to, he were then doing "like a man," as we phrase it. His success, in such case, were complete, his felicity a maximum. This path, to find this path, and walk in it, is the one thing needful for him.

—Thomas Carlyle

The talent of success is nothing more than doing what you can do well; and doing well whatever you do, without a single thought of fame.

—Henry Wadsworth Longfellow

A wise man will make more opportunities than he finds.

—Francis Bacon

If you want a thing done, do it yourself.

—Jean Jacques Rousseau

No bird soars too high, if he soars with his own wings.

—William Blake

What the superior man seeks is in himself: what the small man seeks is in others.

—La Rochefoucauld

Chiefly, the mould of a man's fortune is in his own hands.

—Francis Bacon

DO WHAT YOU CAN

The weakest among us has a gift, however seemingly trivial, which is peculiar to him, and which worthily used, will be a gift also to his race.

—John Ruskin

Hide not your talents, they for use were made. What's a Sun-dial in the Shade?

—Benjamin Franklin

Use what talents you possess; the woods would be very silent if no birds sang there except those that sang best.

—Henry van Dyke

We should not judge of a man's merit by his good qualities, but by the use he can make of them.

—La Rochefoucauld

Doing little things with a strong desire to
please God makes them really great.

—*St. Francis de Sales*

Whatever you do, work at it with all your
heart, as working for the Lord...

Colossians 3:23 (NIV)

It is true that we shall not be able to reach
perfection, but in our struggle toward it we
shall strengthen our characters and give stability
to our ideas, so that, whilst ever advancing
calmly in the same direction, we shall be
rendered capable of applying the faculties with
which we have been gifted to the best possible
account.

—*Confucius*

If you can't be a pine on the top of the hill,
Be a scrub in the valley—but be
The best little scrub by the side of the rill;
Be a bush if you can't be a tree.

—*Douglas Malloch*

Rebellion against your handicaps gets you nowhere. Self-pity gets you nowhere. One must have the adventurous daring to accept oneself as a bundle of possibilities and undertake the most interesting game in the world—making the most of one's best.

—Harry Emerson Fosdick

It is not by regretting what is irreparable that true work is to be done, but by making the best of what we are. It is not by complaining that we have not the right tools, but by using well the tools we have. What we are, and where we are, is God's providential arrangement—God's doing, though it may be man's misdoing; and the manly and the wise way is to look your disadvantages in the face, and see what can be made of them.

—Frederick W. Robertson

It is the greatest of all mistakes to do nothing because you can only do a little. Do what you can.

—Sydney Smith

A man would do nothing, if he waited until he
could do it so well that no one would find fault
with what he has done.

—Cardinal John Henry Newman

It is better to light one small candle than to
curse the darkness.

—Confucius

If the world seems cold to you,
Kindle fires to warm it!

—Lucy Larcom

It is ridiculous for any man to criticize the
works of another if he has not distinguished
himself by his own performance.

—Joseph Addison

Live and learn,
Not first learn and then live.

—Robert Browning

It is not the critic who counts; not the man who points out how the strong man stumbled or where the doer of deeds could have done them better. The credit belongs to the man who is actually in the arena; whose face is marred by dust and sweat and blood; who strives valiantly; who errs, and comes short again and again, because there is no effort without error and shortcoming; who does actually try to do the deed; who knows the great enthusiasm, the great devotion, and spends himself in a worthy cause; who, at the best, knows in the end the triumph of high achievement, and who, at the worst, if he fails, at least fails while daring greatly. Far better is it to dare mighty things, to win glorious triumphs even though checkered by failure, than to rank with those poor spirits who neither enjoy nor suffer much because they live in the gray twilight that knows neither victory nor defeat....Life's a game. Don't flinch, don't foul, and hit that line hard. Play up, play up, and play the game.

—Theodore Roosevelt

Conviction is worthless unless it is converted into conduct.

—Thomas Carlyle

I must lose myself in action, lest I wither in despair.

—Alfred, Lord Tennyson

Life must be measured by thought and action, not by time.

—Sir John Lubbock

If there's a job to be done, I always ask the busiest man in my parish to take it on and it gets done.

—Henry Ward Beecher

If a man knows where to get good advice, it is as though he could supply it himself.

—Johann Wolfgang von Goethe

THE PSALM OF LIFE

Lives of great men all remind us
We can make our lives sublime,
And, departing, leave behind us
Footprints on the sands of time;

Footprints, that perhaps another,
Sailing o'er life's solemn main,
A forlorn and shipwrecked brother,
Seeing, shall take heart again.

Let us, then, be up and doing,
With a heart for any fate;
Still achieving, still pursuing,
Learn to labor and to wait.

—Henry Wadsworth Longfellow

ALL IN THE ATTITUDE

The greatest mistake you can make in this life
is to be continually fearing you will make one.

—Elbert Hubbard

There are people who make no mistakes
because they never try to do anything worth
doing.

—Johann Wolfgang von Goethe

A great deal of talent is lost in this world for
the want of a little courage.

—Author Unknown

I have watched men climb up to success,
hundreds of them, and of all the elements that
are important for success, the most important
is faith. No great thing comes to any man
unless he has courage.

—Cardinal James Gibbons

The hero is no braver than an ordinary man, but he is brave five minutes longer.

—*Ralph Waldo Emerson*

The battle is not to the strong alone; it is to the vigilant, the active, the brave.

—*Patrick Henry*

Quiet minds cannot be perplexed or frightened, but go on in fortune or misfortune at their own private pace, like a clock during a thunderstorm.

—*Robert Louis Stevenson*

We shall steer safely through every storm, so long as our heart is right, our intention fervent, our courage steadfast, and our trust fixed on God. If at times we are somewhat stunned by the tempest, never fear. Let us take breath, and go on afresh.

—*St. Francis de Sales*

A WINNER'S CREED

If you think you are beaten, you are;
If you think you dare not, you don't;
If you'd like to win, but think you can't,
It's almost a cinch you won't.

If you think you'll lose, you're lost,
For out in the world we find
Success begins with a person's faith;
It's all in the state of mind.

Life's battles don't always go
To the stronger or faster hand;
They go to the one who trusts in God
And always thinks "I can."

—*Author Unknown*

Never undervalue yourself. Believe in yourself. Believe that you can do your work well, and then make good. Never doubt yourself. Faith in one's self unlocks those hidden powers that all of us have, but that so few of us use. Every man and woman has undeveloped strength undreamed of until emergencies call it forth. Every one of us has been surprised at how much we can do and how well we can do it when we have to do it.

Do not wait for these emergencies to call out the might within you. Realize your assets every day. God has made an investment in every one of us; shall we go to Him when our life is done giving Him no return upon that investment? When He invested in you He meant that you should pay Him dividends in the betterment of the world and helpfulness to your fellow-men. You can do this only by your best work. And your best work is possible only by faith in yourself and by love of your work.

—*Albert J. Beveridge*

They can conquer who believe they can.
—*Ralph Waldo Emerson*

"Everything is possible for him who believes."
Mark 9:23 (NIV)

Without faith a man can do nothing; with it all things are possible.
—*Sir William Osler*

Our belief at the beginning of a doubtful undertaking is the one thing that insures the successful outcome of our venture.
—*William James*

Self-trust is the first secret of success.
—*Ralph Waldo Emerson*

We must have perseverance and above all confidence in ourselves. We must believe that we are gifted for something...

—Marie Curie

Self-confidence is the first requisite to great undertakings.

—Samuel Johnson

Doubt whom you will, but never yourself.
—Christian Bovee

Be sure you're right, then go ahead.
—Davy Crockett

Let none falter, who thinks he is right, and we may succeed.

—Abraham Lincoln

When love and skill work together, expect a masterpiece.

—John Ruskin

...if one advances confidently in the direction of his dreams, and endeavors to live the life which he has imagined, he will meet with a success unexpected in common hours.

—Henry David Thoreau

Nothing great was ever achieved without enthusiasm.

—Ralph Waldo Emerson

In order to do great things, one must be enthusiastic.

—Louis de Rouvroy

The men whom I have seen succeed have always been cheerful and hopeful, who went about their business with a smile on their faces, and took the changes and chances of this mortal life like men.

—Charles Kingsley

A MATTER OF TIME

Ordinary people merely think how they shall
spend their time; a man of talent tries to use it.

—Arthur Schopenhauer

We always have time enough, if we will but
use it aright.

—Johann Wolfgang von Goethe

This time, like all other times, is a very good
one, if we but know what to do with it.

—Ralph Waldo Emerson

Waste neither time nor money, but make the
best use of both.

—Benjamin Franklin

Make the most of time, it flies away so fast;
yet method will teach you to win time.

—Johann Wolfgang von Goethe

You have to live on this twenty-four hours of daily time. Out of it you have to spin health, pleasure, money, content, respect, and the evolution of your immortal soul. Its right use, its most effective use, is a matter of the highest urgency and of the most thrilling actuality. All depends on that.

—Arnold Bennett

Dost thou love life? Then do not squander time; for that's the stuff life is made of. If time be of all things the most precious, wasting time must be the greatest prodigality; since lost time is never found again and what we call time enough always proves little enough. Let us then be up and doing, and doing to the purpose; so by diligence shall we do more with less perplexity. Sloth makes all things difficult, but industry all easy. Employ thy time well, if thou meanest to gain leisure. Since thou art not sure of a minute, throw not away an hour.

—Benjamin Franklin

Throw away all ambition beyond that of doing the day's work well. The travelers on the road to success live in the present, heedless of taking thought for the morrow. Live neither in the past nor in the future, but let each day's work absorb your entire energies, and satisfy your widest ambition.

—*Sir William Osler*

...today well-lived makes every yesterday a dream of happiness and every tomorrow a vision of hope.

—*from the Sanskrit*

Like the star that shines afar,
Without haste and without rest,
Let each man wheel with steady sway
Round the task that rules the day
And do his best.

—*Johann Wolfgang von Goethe*

Write it on your heart that every day is the best day in the year. No man has learned anything rightly until he knows that every day is doomsday. Today is a king in disguise. Today always looks mean to the thoughtless, in the face of a uniform experience that all good and great and happy actions are made up precisely of these blank todays. Let us not be so deceived; let us unmask the king as he passes.

He only is rich who owns the day, and no one owns the day who allows it to be invaded with worry, fret and anxiety. Finish every day and be done with it. You have done what you could. Some blunders and absurdities no doubt crept in; forget them as soon as you can. Tomorrow is a new day; begin it well and serenely and with too high a spirit to be cumbered with your old nonsense. This day is all that is good and fair. It is too dear, with its hopes and invitations, to waste a moment on the yesterdays.

—*Ralph Waldo Emerson*

Have courage for the great sorrows of life and patience for the small ones; and when you have laboriously accomplished your daily task, go to sleep in peace. God is awake.

—*Victor Hugo*

Would'st shape a noble life? Then cast
No backward glances toward the past,
And though somewhat be lost and gone,
Yet do thou act as one new-born;
What each day needs, that shalt thou ask,
Each day will set its proper task.

—*Johann Wolfgang von Goethe*

One thing at a time, and all things in succession. That which grows slowly endures.

—*Josiah G. Holland*

Our life is frittered away by detail. An honest man has hardly need to count more than his ten fingers, or in extreme cases he may add his ten toes, and lump the rest. Simplicity, simplicity, simplicity! I say, let your affairs be as two or three, and not a hundred or a thousand; instead of a million count half a dozen, and keep your accounts on your thumbnail. In the midst of this chopping sea of civilized life, such are the clouds and storms and quicksands and thousand-and-one items to be allowed for, that a man has to live, if he would not founder and go to the bottom and not make his port at all, by dead reckoning, and he must be a great calculator indeed who succeeds. Simplify, simplify...

—Henry David Thoreau

Use well the moment; what the hour
Brings for thy use is in thy power;
And what thou best canst understand
Is just the thing lies nearest to thy hand.
—*Johann Wolfgang von Goethe*

If thou workest at that which is before thee,
following right reason seriously, vigorously,
calmly, without allowing anything else to
distract thee, but keeping thy divine part sure,
if thou shouldst be bound to give it back
immediately; if thou holdest to this, expecting
nothing, fearing nothing, but satisfied with thy
present activity according to Nature, and with
heroic truth in every word and sound which
thou utterest, thou wilt live happy.
—*Marcus Aurelius*

How make your wit and your width to swell?
Do one thing at a time, and do it well.
—*John Stuart Blackie*

Those who attain to any excellence commonly spend life in some one single pursuit, for excellence is not often gained upon easier terms.

—*Samuel Johnson*

Put all good eggs in one basket and then watch that basket.

—*Andrew Carnegie*

The man who succeeds above his fellows is the one who, early in life, clearly discerns his object, and towards that object habitually directs his powers.

—*Edward Bulwer-Lytton*

I believe the true road to preeminent success in any line is to make yourself master of that line.

—*Andrew Carnegie*

He who every morning plans the transactions of the day and follows out that plan carries a thread that will guide him through the labyrinth of the most busy life. The orderly arrangement of his time is like a ray of light which darts itself through all his occupations. But where no plan is laid, where the disposal of time is surrendered merely to the chance of incidents, chaos will soon reign.

—Victor Hugo

Good order is the foundation of all good things.

—Edmund Burke

Forewarned, forearmed; to be prepared is half the victory.

—Miguel de Cervantes

He who is not prepared today will be less so tomorrow.

—Ovid

Besides the noble art of getting things done,
there is the noble art of leaving things undone.
The wisdom of life consists in the elimination
of nonessentials.

—Lin Yutang

The art of being wise is the art of knowing
what to overlook.

—William James

Greatness of soul consists not so much in
soaring high and pressing forward, as in
knowing how to adapt and limit oneself.

—Michel de Montaigne

In contemplation as in action, we must distinguish between what may be attained and what
is unattainable. Without this, little can be
achieved, either in life or in knowledge.

—Johann Wolfgang von Goethe

THE SECRET OF SUCCESS

The secret of success is constancy to purpose.
>—*Benjamin Disraeli*

Courage and perseverance have a magical talisman, before which difficulties disappear and obstacles vanish into air.
>—*John Quincy Adams*

Great works are performed not by strength but by perseverance.
>—*Samuel Johnson*

Perseverance is a great element of success. If you only knock long enough and loud enough at the gate, you are sure to wake up somebody.
>—*Henry Wadsworth Longfellow*

There are but two ways which lead to great aims and achievements—energy and perseverance. Energy is a rare gift,—it provokes opposition, hatred, and reaction. But perseverance lies within the affordings of everyone, its power increases with its progress, and it but rarely misses its aim.

—Johann Wolfgang von Goethe

He that can have patience can have what he will.

—Benjamin Franklin

There is no road too long to the man who advances deliberately and without undue haste; there are no honors too distant to the man who prepares himself for them with patience.

—Jean de La Bruyère

Genius is eternal patience.

—Michelangelo

No great thing is created suddenly, any more than a bunch of grapes or a fig. If you tell me that you desire a fig, I answer you that there must be time. Let it first blossom, then bear fruit, then ripen.

—Epictetus

To go fast, go slow.
—Elbert Hubbard

Be not afraid of going slowly; be afraid only of standing still.

—Chinese Proverb

Heaven is not reached at a single bound;
But we build the ladder by which we rise
From the lowly earth to the vaulted skies,
And we mount to its summit round by round.
—Josiah G. Holland

Excellence is never granted to man but as the reward of labor.

—*Sir Joshua Reynolds*

It is only through labor and painful effort, by grim energy and resolute courage, that we move on to better things.

—*Theodore Roosevelt*

Drudgery is as necessary to call out the treasures of the mind as harrowing and planting those of the earth.

—*Margaret Fuller*

If you have genius, industry will improve it; if you have none, industry will supply its place.

—*Sir Joshua Reynolds*

Few things are impossible to diligence and skill.

—*Samuel Johnson*

If thou believest a thing impossible, thy despondency shall make it so; but he that persevereth, shall overcome all difficulties.

—Philip Dormer Stanhope

There is no great achievement that is not the result of patient working and waiting.

—Josiah G. Holland

The heights by great men reached and kept
Were not attained by sudden flight,
But they, while their companions slept
Were toiling upward in the night.

—Henry Wadsworth Longfellow

The most disastrous times have produced the greatest minds. The purest metal comes of the most ardent furnace, the most brilliant lightning comes of the darkest clouds.

—Chateaubriand

Great things are done when men and mountains meet.

—*William Blake*

The gem cannot be polished without friction, nor man perfected without trials.

—*Confucius*

Life affords no higher pleasure than that of surmounting difficulties, passing from one step of success to another, forming new wishes, and seeing them gratified. He that labors in any great or laudable undertaking has his fatigues first supported by hope, and afterwards rewarded by joy...To strive with difficulties, and to conquer them, is the highest human felicity.

—*Samuel Johnson*

Difficulties are the things that show what men are.

—*Epictetus*

I have learned that success is to be measured not so much by the position that one has reached in life as by the obstacles which he has overcome while trying to succeed.

—*Booker T. Washington*

Nothing is such an obstacle to the production of excellence as the power of producing what is good with ease and rapidity.

—*John Aikin*

People do not lack strength; they lack will.

—*Victor Hugo*

...it is for want of application, rather than means, that men fail of success.

—*La Rochefoucauld*

Never despair. But if you do, work on in despair.

—*Edmund Burke*

DON'T QUIT

Don't quit when the tide is lowest,
For it's just about to turn;
Don't quit over doubts and questions,
For there's something you may learn.

Don't quit when the night is darkest,
For it's just a while 'til dawn;
Don't quit when you've run the farthest,
For the race is almost won.

Don't quit when the hill is steepest,
For your goal is almost nigh;
Don't quit, for you're not a failure
Until you fail to try.

—Jill Wolf

Never give up! If adversity presses,
Providence wisely has mingled the cup,
And the best counsel, in all your distresses,
Is the stout watchword of "Never give up."
—Martin F. Tupper

Our greatest glory is not in never falling, but in
rising every time we fall.

—Oliver Goldsmith

To dry one's eyes and laugh at a fall,
And baffled, get up and begin again.
—Robert Browning

There is no failure except in no longer trying.
—Elbert Hubbard

It is no disgrace to start all over. It is usually an
opportunity.

—George Matthew Adams